The Seeing Eye

written by Emily North
illustrated by Rae Ecklund

McGraw-Hill School Division
New York Farmington

Dorothy Harrison Eustis lived in Switzerland in the 1920s. She studied German shepherds. She learned that they were brave, smart, and loyal dogs.

Dorothy trained German shepherds to work with the army and police. She wondered what else they could do.

In 1927 Dorothy heard about a school in Germany that trained German shepherds to help the blind. It had been started to help soldiers who were blinded in battle.

Dorothy wanted to see the school for herself, so she traveled to Germany.

Dorothy was excited when she saw what was happening at the school. The dogs helped the blind men to be brave and confident.

One man took Dorothy on a tour of the city with his dog. She was amazed at the way the dog stopped at curbs and led its owner through crowds and traffic.

Dorothy wanted the whole world to know about these German shepherds. She wrote an article about the wonderful guide dogs that helped blind men "see."

A young blind man named Morris Frank read the article. He knew that having one of these special guide dogs could change his life.

Morris wrote a letter to Dorothy. He told her there were no guide dogs in America. She invited him to come to the school in Germany.

When Morris arrived, he met Buddy, the dog who would be his friend and guide.

First Morris learned to walk with Buddy.

Buddy wore a stiff, U-shaped harness that helped him feel what Morris wanted him to do. But Morris also had to learn to listen to Buddy.

One day, Morris and Buddy took a cable car into town. They got off at the station.

Buddy stepped in front of Morris to let him know there were steps ahead of them. But Morris didn't listen. He slipped and fell down the steps. He wasn't hurt, but he now knew that listening to Buddy would keep him from having accidents.

Morris knew that his life had changed. With Buddy, Morris could now go anywhere.

Soon it was time for Morris and Buddy to go home to Nashville, Tennessee. As they traveled home, Morris showed audiences what he and Buddy could do. The crowds cheered.

Morris wanted to start an American school to train dogs to help the blind. In 1929, his dream came true. Dorothy and some teachers from the school in Germany came to help. Morris named his school The Seeing Eye.

In 1931, the school moved to Morristown, New Jersey. It is still there today.

All the dogs go through the same training. First puppies go to live with families. There they learn to love and be friendly with people. They play and explore the world.

When they go back to the school, they learn basic commands like "Sit!" and "Stay!" They learn to walk with the same kind of U-shaped harness that Buddy wore.

Then trainers walk them on quiet streets. The dogs learn to stop at curbs and watch for cars.

The dogs look out for hidden dangers. They have to lead the person away from places that seem safe, but really aren't.

They learn that what is okay for a dog might not be for a person. A branch that is above a dog's head might hit the dog's taller owner.

The big test is the busy streets of Morristown. There the dogs have to take their trainers through crowds and traffic. They learn to behave in stores and restaurants.

When a dog passes all these tests, it is ready to guide a blind person.

The new owner stays at the school for a month to practice with the new dog. It can be a hard time. The dog must get used to a complete stranger. The owner must learn to feed the dog and wipe off its coat.

Most important, new owners must allow the dogs to guide them. The owner and the dog must learn to trust one another.

After a lot of practice, the dog and owner become a team. Their lives are changed.

The Seeing Eye has joined nearly 12,000 dogs with blind men and women. Thanks to Morris and Buddy, many blind people are now able to make their dreams come true.